HER JOURNEY THROUGH MY EYES

ROBERT ATTENELLO

ARCHWAY
PUBLISHING

Archway Publishing books may be ordered through booksellers or by contacting:

Archway Publishing
1663 Liberty Drive
Bloomington, IN 47403
www.archwaypublishing.com
844-669-3957

ISBN: 978-1-6657-0613-1 (sc)
ISBN: 978-1-6657-0612-4 (hc)
ISBN: 978-1-6657-0614-8 (e)

Library of Congress Control Number: 2021908257

Print information available on the last page.

Archway Publishing rev. date: 06/07/2021

This book is dedicated to the loving memory
of my wonderful wife, Lillian, and to all
the loved ones involved in caring for a
cancer patient, from beginning to end.

ACKNOWLEDGMENTS

Special thanks, love, and appreciation to:

Ken and Terri, for always being there for Lillian and me, and for putting together such memorable events.

Sal and Susan, for keeping me glued together, and for always making Lillian and me laugh.

Pat and Pam, for their thoughts and prayers throughout Lillian's battle.

Mrs. Pat, for her kind tenderness, spiritual guidance, and warm visits.

Dave and Sue, for all that they did for us, and for Sue's help during Lillian's final days.

Kara and Mark, for all their support and love.

Bonnie, for always reaching out to Lillian, making her smile, and showing her all her latest cake creations.

Special thanks to Lillian's brother, Ralph Jr., for making the plane flight several times to spend valuable time with Lillian and me in true support.

And most importantly, a very special thanks to my attorney, David Baram, for introducing me to the most beautiful and sweetest woman in the world.

And to everyone who helped us along the way and gave us so much loving support.

INTRODUCTION

This book is a true love story about two ordinary people—he a construction worker and estimator, she a real estate and immigration paralegal. Bobby loved Lillian for twenty-three years before a tragic diagnosis took the love of his life away. This story dives deep into wonderful memories and meaningful events throughout their life together, and includes her three-year courageous battle with breast cancer.

After reading *Her Journey through My Eyes*, I hope that you will always appreciate the simple things in your life and never look too far ahead. Don't take any day on this earth for granted, and enjoy each day to its fullest. Most of all, if you or a loved one are ever faced with a terminal diagnosis, I hope this book will give you better insight into what to expect.

HOW WE BEGAN

I t was late spring of 1997. My niece Lynn and I were at our monthly scheduled appointment with my attorney, David Baram, at his office to go over some business issues.

As we sat waiting for our appointment, I heard the click-clack of high heels coming down the hallway toward the lobby. I turned my head and noticed a beautiful dark-haired woman in a red skirt with a white blouse and dark blue, high-heeled pumps. My God, she knocked me off my feet! I turned to my niece and asked, "Who the hell is that fine-looking woman?"

Lynn laughed and said, "Uncle Bob, that's Lillian!"

I replied, "That's the same Lillian I deal with from accounts payable?"

Lynn again laughed and said, "Yes that's her!" We then were called in for our appointment.

As soon as I was seated in front of my attorney, I asked him where the hell they had been hiding Lillian all the years we'd been doing business with the firm. He laughed and told me she had an office in the back and usually didn't come out front. I asked him to please introduce me to her. I told him, "She is gorgeous!"

He then told me that she was "very athletic and very emotional at times." He went on to say, "You probably wouldn't get along with her," as he laughed. But at my request, he asked her to please come in, and he introduced us. I stood up to offer her my hand.

As she shook it, she said, "I know who you are Mr. Attenello. Very nice to finally meet you."

My heart was pounding hard and fast in my chest. I believe I fell in love with her right then and there. I'm not a big believer in the old cliché of love at first sight, but I definitely did have some kind of spell cast over me that day, and I believe that it will last forever.

Over the next few weeks, I spoke with Lillian on the phone frequently. I used any and every reason I could think of to talk to her. I eventually gave her my pager number so she could talk to me anytime. We discovered that both she and I were at the tail end of our current marriages. I had filed for divorce and was separated, and Lillian was about to go through the same process. We had discussed how hard it was because of the kids. She had two and I had three, and like most parents, we worried about the impact of our divorces on them.

After a few months, we eventually agreed to meet for a glass of wine at a local restaurant and chat about what we were going through. I discovered that Lillian was a wonderful woman, a very good mother, and most of all, a very interesting person to talk to. We both quickly realized how much we had in common; we were raised the same, with the same values and beliefs.

Like my attorney had said, Lillian was indeed athletic and knowledgeable about every kind of sport imaginable, and we came to realize that we rooted for all the same teams. We continued to talk often by phone, and met a couple more times for lunches and dinners and discussed everyday things. We were both committed to our children and to the reality of the long road ahead of us in ending our lives as we knew it with our spouses before we could think about starting a new relationship.

Soon I realized that I loved and cared about Lillian. It was like we had known each other forever. I loved talking to her, spending time with her, and most of all, just hearing her voice. I valued her opinions on all the subjects that we discussed. This is the way our relationship continued. After a while we both became frustrated that we couldn't have more from our relationship or each other. I guess some people would classify it as a love affair, but I say it was faith, or at least an introduction of a developing friendship that bloomed into a loving relationship between two people who fell deeply in love.

Both Lillian and I were determined to keep respect and dignity for each other's children during our dissolving marriages. We became each other's support in our parenting obligations. At times, this would prove to be challenging due to our scheduled time being interrupted or canceled. Through all the trials and tribulations, we stayed very loyal and dedicated to each other and our blooming relationship. The one thing that we did know is that we didn't want to be without each other, and enjoyed being together more than anything in the world.

In time, we introduced our kids. They all blended naturally. We did family activities with our kids. They all seemed to really get along. We tried to schedule our children to be with their other parent during the same times, which helped us to balance out the romantic side of our relationship, while devoting time to our own individual parenting duties as well.

When Lillian and I could spend weekends alone

together, it always seemed like a holiday, it was so special. We ate dinners out and did fun things together during the day. The one thing that I can honestly say is that we really enjoyed making love to each other. It was so passionate and blissful, like nothing I've ever experienced in a relationship before.

One of the first things that Lillian introduced me to was long weekends at Wildwood Beach in New Jersey. We would spend our days beginning with early morning jogs along the beach, followed by a full day of basking in the sun and enjoying body surfing in the waves. Lillian, a pillar of strength and true athleticism, was always challenging me to see who could ride the waves the furthest.

Around sundown, we would head to our second-floor beach front room to shower and get ready for date night in Cape May. We could never just shower and go; we took time to make passionate love to each other first, and those are the memories that I will always cherish. At dinner, we would hold hands while sitting across from each other. That type of handholding was the way it always was throughout all the years we were together.

Lillian had an outrageously fun and zany personality, always joking and having fun. She was a total blast to be with. I'll never forget one morning, we were up early having coffee on the hotel balcony of our room when we noticed a troller about a quarter mile out. We were both looking through binoculars, and we decided that the boat and its crew were trying to save a whale. After close to an hour, we realized that they were only shrimping. It was quite a letdown, and we laughed all morning long about that.

The next day, Lillian and I took a four-mile walk into town on the bay side of Wildwood to shop for a new bathing suit for me. Back then, I'm embarrassed to say, I use to wear Speedos for swim trunks. She took me to a well-known surf and swim shop, insisting that I go into the men's dressing room to try on three pairs of Speedos. While I was in the room trying on the Speedos, Lillian walked across the street into another shop to use their restroom, leaving me in the dressing room talking to her, thinking she was still outside the dressing room door. When she returned with me still in the dressing room trying on the last Speedo, I thought she would still be out there. Unbeknownst to me, I was now chatting away with whomever was standing outside the door, and not Lillian as I thought. My sweetheart Lillian stood about forty feet away as I came out in the new Speedo in front of several strangers, all laughing their heads off, including Lillian, of course.

Another time, we went out to eat late one evening to a pasta and pizza all you can eat. By the time we were done eating, my stomach began bubbling. I quickly paid the bill and hauled ass for the door. Lillian drove so damn slow, hitting every red light between the restaurant and our hotel room. When we were about one block away, I jumped out and ran for our room. I could hear Lillian laughing while she pulled into the parking lot behind me. Like I said, she was a joker sometimes. As the years went by, we always continued our yearly vacations to Wildwood Beach. Every year proved to be as fun and romantic as all the past ones.

For the first years of our relationship we kept our separate residences, hers being a couple of towns away. We would often spend weekends doing things together with our kids. I give credit to Lillian for being the true staple of our families. She always lit up any room with her humorous personality. One thing that everyone closest to Lillian knew was that she was from old school values and a hard love kind of woman, with a heart larger than life itself—family was always her first priority.

During the winter, we would snowboard at local ski slopes with all of our kids. Lillian would stay in the lodge making lunches and tending to all of our needs. By the second season, we had her on a snowboard enjoying the sport with the rest of us. My oldest son, Bobby Jr., was extremely good at the sport. In no time at all he had taught Lillian to ride, and she was riding her board down the slopes with no trouble at all. On some weekends, we would take all five kids to Vermont's bigger ski resort, and as always, she would be the mother hen; but she also got to enjoy a few trips down the slopes with me. We always enjoyed the long ride up on the chair lifts talking, kissing, and holding each other close.

One thing that you will constantly read throughout my story is how much loving affection Lillian and I had for each other. No matter what we were doing, our love for each other would always shine through.

Lillian always was a mom first to all of our kids. One memory will always stand out as truth of that. My second oldest son Danny, who is special needs, was snowboarding with all of us. When we decided to break for lunch, we noticed he was missing from our group. Lillian was upset and worried, and was searching the lower slopes. When she finally found Danny, he was enjoying one last ride on the bunny hill before joining us in the lodge for lunch. When he and Lillian came in together, she was crying her eyes out. We worked to calm her down, trying to explain that he knew his way around and she shouldn't worry so much.

Lillian had a very sensitive and kind heart, which was on full display. She was a wonderful mother and more importantly, the best girlfriend, and eventually wife, a man could ever have. So loyal, dedicated, and loving.

Several years into our relationship, things became unsettled and complicated between us due to her children's constant needs. Her son had gotten very involved in soccer and required shuttling back and forth to his practices and games. This took up most of her time, both after work and on weekends. This went on for a long while. I felt harsh in the way I was starting to feel about Lillian's constant accommodations and extreme involvement in every activity that her son had. It was hard on both of us. She and I talked about it constantly. She tried everything possible to balance our relationship, but we had canceled so many trips to the beach on weekends, not to mention countless dinner plans.

During that winter, I can remember snowboarding trips that would be postponed or canceled because of the last-minute changes involving her children's activities. I was hurt, disappointed, and at times, pissed off. I had a very hard time understanding why Lillian couldn't figure out a way to better balance our relationship and have me feel like I was a significant part of her life.

As time went on, I started to question our love for

each other. I knew I loved her more than anything, but maybe this was her way of helping me to realize I might not be the right man for her; or maybe she was testing to see how much I would accept and deal with. There were many harsh conversations and uneasy situations until I finally called it quits with her and our relationship. We were both heartbroken. For months, we tried to just be friends and would go out now and then for a bite to eat. It became very disheartening and frustrating for both of us.

We finally agreed to go our separate ways. I admit that I resented the whole situation, but I moved on. In my opinion, Lillian didn't get much help from her ex-husband in after-school or weekend activities, which left her no choice but to do all of it herself.

After a few months, I started seeing another woman, which really hurt Lillian and made me feel awful. I ended the casual relationship within a month. I had a hard time being with anyone else other than my sweetheart, Lillian.

During our separation, my son Bobby Jr. and I got into motocross and began racing the New England circuit. Bobby and I both made good friendships and found we enjoyed racing. I never stopped loving and thinking about Lillian. I would check my phone every morning and every night to see if she had called or left me a message. It hurt like hell not being with her, and I often wondered if she was missing me as much as I missed her. I had more opportunities to date here and there, but could never bring myself to do it. I realized that my heart, body, and soul belonged to Lillian—it was way beyond my control.

Months went by with very little communication from her, if any at all. I am a very headstrong individual who tries to control myself and all my surroundings. Sometimes my temper would get the best of me because I couldn't control this situation. Bobby Jr. once said to me, "Dad, you're weak when it comes to that woman!" and he was 100 percent correct. I knew one thing for sure, I never wanted to be without her. I stood my ground and tried to move on with my life without her being a major part of it.

One night around 11:00 p.m. my home phone rang. I answered it to hear Lillian's wonderful voice say, "Hello Bobby," in a very soft hesitant way.

There was complete silence for almost a minute until I finally choked out, "Sweetheart, I love you and miss you so much, it's good to hear your voice," followed by another silent moment. Then I heard Lillian softly crying as she told me she loved me more than anything in the world and didn't want to live without me another day in her life. We both wept openly.

After a time, I told her that we really needed to have a long conversation about what was needed in our relationship in order for it to work. I told her the deep love we had for each other and our compatibility was not, and would never be, a problem. We agreed to meet that following weekend to talk over helpful changes in how we could handle our relationship moving forward.

That weekend our plan to get together once again failed due to her son's shuttling and other unexpected events. Lillian called me on Sunday night when her kids were finally with their dad. Our phone conversation began with me telling her that it was never going to work out between us. That I was not the type of guy who would wait in line until she finally got to me. I went on to tell her that I respected her loyalty and dedication as a mother toward her children, but hers was way over the top and totally out of control. I insisted that without help from her ex-husband, she'd never have a good relationship with any man. I gave my own situation as an example of how their mother and I balanced out the responsibilities and respected each other's private lives. I told her in a harsh tone that it was time for her to listen or to spend the rest of her life alone, catering to her children's every need. I went on to explain that one day they'd leave the nest to live their own lives, and she'd find herself alone wondering what might have been; how different her life might be if she chose managing our relationship better, or respecting our true love for each other, instead of being a constant shuttle service for her kids. I also told her that all her children's youth adventures might not amount to anything, but would force her to be alone. Lillian told me that she didn't know what else to do, her ex-husband would not make the time to do it. I told her, "And that's my point, you don't get any support!"

We were both crying because we both knew that what I was saying had a lot of truth to it. I told her she needed to make changes in her life; that it was time to hold someone else accountable, to share the responsibilities so she could have a life. Before Lillian could speak another word, I told her in the calmest voice I could that she should take a week or longer and figure it out, then make whatever, if any, changes to see how things go. I told her if she chose *us*, with a much better-balanced relationship and quality time with me as her final decision, then she needed to stand firm by it. I then said, "Call me in a while after you choose the direction you want to go in." That was the end of our phone conversation.

I didn't sleep that night or many nights following. I knew it was harsh of me, but I needed to speak for me as her lover or it would never last, and we would be right back in the same situation. A couple of long weeks went by. I assumed that she ignored our conversation and moved on with her life as is.

To my surprise, one evening she called me. I thought the worst, that she was going to tell me goodbye once again. She said, "Hi Bobby, please let me talk first, then when I'm done, you can have the floor." She went on to say, "I've done a lot of thinking and a lot of true soul searching, thinking about everything you said. I love my two kids and want to be there for them, but I want you and I to be together. I can't live with myself thinking of what could have been between us because I already know I love you and how much you love me, and I know we'll always be together. We have such a loving relationship and love being together more than anything in the world. You're the most important thing in my life, and I never want to lose you. And so, I will balance my commitments so we can spend more time together, I promise." She also said that it wasn't only because of what I had told her, but it was the right thing to do. All I could do was tell her how much I loved her, and thanked her for the decision she had chosen to make.

The following weekend we were together again and thoroughly enjoyed each other's company. We had a romantic weekend, including dinners out and a day at the beach. It had never felt so good to finally be in each other's arms, making love, and sharing the same bed. We were on cloud nine.

Reflecting back to this bump in our relationship, it must have been eight months or more before we were back together. It was like we hit the light switch back to the *on* position—our relationship and love for each other just kept getting better and stronger with very few problems. Our total commitment was even stronger than before. Lillian was a woman of conviction. Whenever she set her mind to something it was always 100 percent, never halfway. She and I continued to love each other unconditionally throughout our years together. I stayed over at her house almost all the time. We started living our lives together, helped each other to meet monthly bills, saved money together, and even adopted and raised a beautiful springer spaniel named Maggie. She was our baby.

As time passed, we purchased our first boat. Every weekend we went to lakes, sometimes with the kids, enjoying the sun and water. Both Lillian and I could operate a boat well, as we both had our boating operator's license. We went to Lake Ontario on a salmon fishing trip, caught some big king salmon that were the best we ever ate. Lillian could reel in the big fish and was an excellent first mate. Anything we did together was a competition, but always just for fun. And what fun it was. I found that Lillian was somewhat of a tomboy, but still had a beautiful feminine side to her. A man couldn't have asked for a better loving soulmate than her. I feel extremely lucky and truly blessed to have had Lillian in my life.

During the year 2002, I sold my epoxy floor business. It wasn't doing the volume of business I expected, and it was very stressful, and costing me money, just trying to keep it afloat. I went back to work with the tools of my trade as a concrete mason and did pretty well for a number of years. Eventually, I turned the company over to my oldest son, Bobby Jr. He was a smart businessman, and in no time, grew the company even more and increased the volume of work to a whole new level. Lillian and I could not have been prouder of him.

She always had a strong connection with Bobby, Jr. She told me throughout the years of our relationship that he was her favorite. There was no disrespect meant to her own children, they just had a little-brother / big-sister-type connection. He was always there for us, and with us in good times and bad, throughout our entire relationship. Back when Bobby Jr. and I raced motocross and would sometimes get hurt pretty badly, it was "Mama Lillian" who said enough is enough, you both are done! And we listened. She would have that "conviction" in her tone.

Life calmed down for us and soon shifted toward a finer and slower pace. I was finally over being a bit on the wild side. I followed her lead and she introduced me to hiking. Not your average slow hike through the woods, more like the aggressive style of hiking up mountains, hills, and along ledge-covered terrain. Our average hike was at least five miles, sometimes up to seven, and of course, this had to be done in record time with short water breaks for us and our dogs. This was traditionally what we did Saturday or Sunday mornings.

We pushed and supported each other to the very best that we could be, no matter what it entailed, right down to our work ethic. Lillian taught me to give 100 percent at work, personal chores, projects, and all other activities. When I first met Lillian, I was conceited, somewhat of a pompous ass, and could be a loose cannon. Throughout the years, she somehow calmed me down and taught me how to think before I acted. She taught me to look at the positive side of situations, and more importantly, showed me unconditional love, which is what I had for her. People would naturally gravitate to Lillian. She was a very interesting and unique woman, with a zany side to her, and pretty as hell. She always kept us active.

Her biggest passion was being on the water, boating, and saltwater fishing. She was involved in sailing growing up. Being out on the water all day was natural for her. We would drop anchor at the lake or in the bay, watch the sunset, sip wine, hold hands, and chat. We both enjoyed every precious moment we had together, and we weren't ashamed to proclaim that to each other every day.

There was a balance in our active lifestyle. There would be weekends that we would opt to stay home and relax. We would cook nice dinners—make homemade pasta and sauce—watch a good movie together, or just sit on our back deck talking or enjoying an occasional bonfire in the evenings. No matter what we chose to do, it was always romantic. The love we shared for one another helped me realize that the most rewarding and beautiful things in life come in the simplest of packages. This was one of Lillian's biggest legacies, the way she could bring out the best of qualities in a person.

I remember golfing with her. I was winning by several strokes, which was an unusual situation because she was a very good golfer. On the back nine with only a few more holes to go, she decided to throw me off my game— waiting until I was about to tee off and pulling up her shirt to flash me. The rest of the game went downhill for me and she beat me by a single stroke. She was a lot of fun to be around and very zany at times, and that was one of the many things I loved about her.

Eventually, Lillian and I decided to live together, just as a married couple would. She felt it made absolutely no sense for us to live apart when we spent almost all of our weekends, and many work nights, together at each other's houses. We looked at several houses in the Granby and East Granby area, but finally decided that we would live together in her house.

We shared all the financial obligations and had joint checking and savings accounts. We invested a lot of money into upgrades and renovations of our together home. Our plan was five years of outdoor and indoor interior renovations, which we did mostly ourselves. We made an awesome team. I did all the construction and landscaping, with much of her help. She managed all the financials as well as the weekly and monthly bills.

We began by landscaping the backyard, clearing trees, remaking the flower beds, and reseeding the lawn. Lillian and I cleared out about a quarter acre of woods to give more room for our two springer spaniel dogs, Marshall and Molly, to run. We enclosed the entire backyard with a four-foot fence. We removed the asphalt front walkway and installed a brick paver walk, using nothing more than a sledgehammer, pickaxe, and hand tamper. Lillian wheeled each and every piece of broken asphalt up our backyard hill to a low area to use as fill. This woman was tougher than most men I worked with. I loved doing home projects with her. Her strength and stamina amazed me.

Our next home project was to completely remodel our kitchen and dining room into a combo country kitchen. We removed the divider wall that separated the rooms and opened everything up into one big room, tiled the kitchen floor, and installed a new island. Bobby, Jr. installed the new counter tops and sink. We both loved the results. Kitchen cabinets would come later, after we had saved money for that upgrade. We started painting one room at a time and eventually had every room throughout the entire house, upstairs and downstairs, completed. We remodeled and upgraded the finished basement, installing a small bar area and big screen television as well as an electric fireplace, which heated the space very well.

Over the next couple of years, we replaced all the furniture in the entire house from the basement to the bedrooms upstairs. We had new carpets installed throughout the upstairs bedrooms and hallway. On year three of our plan, we had ductless AC and a new heating system installed. At that point, Lillian sat me down and strongly suggested that I should consider being quitclaimed on the deed. I responded with "No, thanks."

I liked it the way it was. She kept on me about doing it for over a year.

To help convince me, she created a simple spreadsheet recording everything I did renovation wise, from my labor and money spent for the upgrades and remodeling projects, to taking out a loan for the AC and heating-system upgrade. She came up with a large dollar figure, which was almost as much as half the equity amount of the house. She also went on about the amount of money spent over the years of me paying a part of the mortgage and utilities, etc. I finally said, "Yes, this makes sense. And if it makes you happy, I'll do it."

Lillian was also thinking ahead. The next thing she suggested was for us to see an insurance agent that she knew and trusted in order to purchase life insurance for ourselves. That took a lot of convincing—it kind of creeped me out—but because it was Lillian, I followed her lead, and we did it. Her words to me were, "If one of us loses the other, it will no doubt be the most devasting and heartbreaking experience for us to deal with. So, let's at least be able to have the money to live on." This would prove to be another smart choice that Lillian made. I thought that, after all, I would never want to leave her sad and broke. I always felt and truly believed that I would die first, being a bit older than her and being worn down from all my years in construction and the years of competitive bodybuilding.

We loved to leash walk our dogs after work through our neighborhood. We would have some of our best conversations during these walks. Here, I often learned of the deeper spiritual side of Lillian. (I always knew she was a good Christian, as we would often go to church together.) There was one conversation that will always stand in the forefront of my mind. On a fall evening, we were on one of our walks. Lillian was intently listening to me carry on about how I wished we had a lot of money to do whatever we wanted and never have to worry about our budget bills. Lillian was quietly listening to me vent my frustrations. When I was all done, she said, "Bobby, don't waste your time being greedy, trying to pick the daily fruit that life has to offer. Instead, be thankful for what we have as you nurture the tree it grows on."

I fell quiet and thought about what she was trying to say. I realized that she was referring to the love we had for each other and the well-balanced, simple life we shared together, and to trust that good things would come our way. This was one way that Lillian changed me to be a better man, a more sensitive and calmer person. I always listened and took to heart her soft words during these very intimate, personal conversations. She never gave up on me, or on us, or in all we believed in. I always felt that Lillian never had to lean on me. I never overshadowed her, nor she me. But the reality is that she was the true backbone of our relationship. She always showed me how to remain positive in everything and never give up in any situation. No one, not our families, friends, or even our kids, knew Lillian better than me or knew me better than Lillian did.

Lillian loved all the holidays. When Halloween was only a few weeks away, she would get pumpkins, cornstalks, and scarecrows and decorate the front yard. She loved to decorate the family room and kitchen with seasonal orange candles and small figurines, in true spirit of the holiday. She would bake her homemade apple crisp and pumpkin pies, and have fresh ground pumpkin spice coffee every morning. She loved the change of seasons. She was a fanatic about all that the fall entails, including raking and leaf blowing. This was our favorite time of the year. Both of us were huge football fans. We would spend every Sunday on an early morning hike with our dogs or a run through our neighborhood. This was followed by a homemade Italian dinner, which we would always enjoy eating during the late-afternoon game. I really enjoyed watching football with Lillian. She knew the rules of the game better than I did. Being curled up on the couch together with food and football was really the only way we would both completely relax.

Thanksgiving was another holiday that Lillian enjoyed. We would celebrate the holiday the Friday after Thanksgiving so all five of our kids could come over and spend time with us. This schedule was best for everybody because there was no competition for the day, as they had no other place to be or people to see. We would cook a huge turkey with all the fixings or sometimes a prime-rib dinner, with Lillian's homemade pies for dessert. We always had a ton of laughs and lots of fun with the house full of guests.

No holiday was more exciting and spiritual to Lillian than Christmas. Our tradition was to go pick our Christmas tree the weekend following Thanksgiving. I was not a huge fan of Christmas, and found it difficult to be excited, but always found myself looking forward to it—to be totally involved in the decorating and all the preparations for the holiday. It was really hard not to catch the excitement while surrounded by Lillian's total joy and enthusiasm for it. (This part of my love story is one of toughest things to write because, once again, Lillian taught me the true spirit and meaning of Christmas. Just one more way that she touched my heart with her subtle ways of teaching.)

In the week following Thanksgiving, both Lillian and I would decorate the house room by room, with Christmas carols softly playing in the background. We would hang lights outside and tiny white lights over the family room and the archway in the living room. I would watch her as she hung the beautifully designed Christmas stockings on our fireplace mantle. We would go into town a few evenings to shop for small, but very thoughtful, gifts for our kids and never forgot to get gifts for our dogs. Lillian did all this with such a joyful and giving heart. I always marveled at how she just adored the Christmas holiday. She wasn't at all about the shopping and gifts, but more about the symbolic meaning and spiritual feeling of this religious holiday.

We would spend Christmas Eve just the two of us, going to church—which to me was the most beautiful service, with a full choir and acoustic guitars—singing Christmas carols, and listening to meaningful readings. Lillian and I would always dress up for this occasion. She would tell me that now was the perfect time to remember what Christmas was all about. We would sit close together holding hands, and I would always have tears in my eyes when the choir sang. She would gently wipe the tears and hold my hand even tighter. I could never explain why I always cried, but she could. She once told me that it was because God was touching my soul.

Before we left the church, we would always light candles for all our loved ones who had passed. Each year when we returned home, we would change into more comfortable clothes and have a bite to eat while planning the Christmas Day meal and activities for our kids. Before bed, I would watch Lillian as she caringly and methodically put gifts into the stockings and placed gifts under the tree. It was so special to watch how much she enjoyed this precious holiday. It was a perfect example of her selfless and caring ways. As I look back now, she taught me that the true spirit of Christmas was to give to others and never think of yourself.

When Christmas Day came, I would quietly get out of bed and sneak downstairs to get Lillian's gifts and her stocking stuffers out of my truck and put them with the other gifts under the tree. She always insisted that she and I not get gifts for each other, but somehow, we always did. At the end of the Christmas Day festivities, when everyone went home, I would lie in bed and reflect on how much she had put herself into this wonderful holiday to make it enjoyable for everyone in a very special way. I would thank God for my biggest Christmas gift, which was to be blessed with the most wonderful, thoughtful, and loving woman that any man could ever have. Amen!

After the holidays were over, both Lillian and I would set our focus on different outdoor activities. We weren't ones to sit around the house after work and on weekends. Time and time again, Lillian would prove to be very athletic, always ready to go. She looked forward to snowy days and enjoyed snowshoeing on fresh snow. This outdoor activity works up one hell of a sweat. When we first got into shoeing, I figured we would snowshoe about a mile, but not when Lillian was involved—we would snowshoe three to four miles. I always had to be my best in order to keep up with her. That was the way she was, always 100 percent at whatever we did. Her favorite saying was "go big or go home." At the end of our snowshoeing hikes, we would be dripping in sweat and my legs would be burning. Our dogs would be panting and ready for a long afternoon nap.

Some nights after work, we would take flashlights and do two- to three-mile runs around the neighborhood, because Lillian hated just doing nothing. She made sure that we always stayed in the mid to upper seven-minute mile range, no matter what. She would say, "If we're running eight-minute miles, we might as well be walking." Of course, this was always said in fun and just to crank me up. But it never did. I was always proud of the way she would push us to do well at everything we did.

She was the toughest woman I ever met. She lived her entire life believing there was always a challenge calling our names and that there was nothing we couldn't overcome. That's the way her life was. No matter what the sport, whether it be strapping into snowshoes, ratcheting into her snowboard or cross-country skis, or even lacing up her sneakers, it always was "game on." I'll never forget her don't-give-up attitude, which she also instilled in me. (I know you are most likely thinking that no woman could ever be this determined, strong, or kindhearted. Lillian was, and that's why I wrote this book.)

Easter was another special holiday for both Lillian and me, not only for the religious and symbolic meaning, but because we considered this to be the start of spring. Weather permitting, we would try to get early spring cleanup done in our backyard. We put all our patio furniture out and set up our outdoor fireplace. Mulch beds would be all fluffed and dusted with fresh mulch and anything else we could complete before the holiday weekend arrived. We would try to take Good Friday off, or at least take a half day, so we could start the process of making our traditional Easter pies. Lillian would set up her Easter decorations, baskets of candy, and colored eggs and plan an awesome spiral-ham dinner. We would begin baking our Easter pies first thing on Saturday morning, because that afternoon we would gather at my sister Terri and brother-in-law Ken's house for a family taste test to see which of our family members made the best looking and tastiest Easter pie. In my opinion, they were all beautiful and delicious. There were always lots of laughs and fun whenever we all got together. Some Easters, Lillian and I would attend Easter service at our local church if time would allow. The day was usually spent at our house with a spiral-ham dinner with Lillian, me, and her two children. It was always a relaxing day with good conversation and a peaceful atmosphere. Our conversations would include the planning and anticipation of summer trips and events.

During the months of April and May, we continued our yard work, planting flowers, hanging plants, and overseeding the front and back lawns. We took great pride in our home, not to keep up with the Joneses but just to keep what we had fresh and well maintained for our enjoyment. We loved working in the yard together. It was one of our biggest enjoyments—being outside and creating an enjoyable outdoor environment. I would love to grab her, hug her, and steal kisses from her because she simply truly amazed me by just being the kind of woman that she was. I'm not ashamed to admit that, neither then, nor now as I write this story.

That's how our "Old Farts Family Barbecue" every Memorial Day began. It was usually just my side of the family with a few good friends added in. It was always a total riot and a complete blast. Everyone always enjoyed our events, and there was always plenty of food and drink. This family tradition started because Lillian wanted to add another get-together with my family. The conversations and shenanigans that went down at our old farts barbecue were totally over the top and absolutely hilarious. When people would leave, from the late afternoon into the evening, they would be walking out the door still laughing over something that my brother, Sal, or I said or did during the day.

Sal and I are the closest of brothers, and we went through everything you could ever imagine brothers going through. Some good times, some bad times, but we always had each other's back. Lillian loved my brother. She said that there was no difference in our personalities and zany humor, not to mention our speech. Lillian and I spent a lot of time with Sal and his wonderful girlfriend, Susan. She balanced his personality and calmed him down a notch or two. That's why I really liked Susan, because of how well she treated my brother, and more importantly, the way they both always made Lillian and I feel welcome and loved in their company. Our Fourth of July weekends were most often spent down by the shoreline with Sal and Susan. During the day, we would spend time at the beach and walk around the quaint town of Niantic. We would also visit the rustic taverns and shops, followed by an awesome outdoor patio dinner and plenty of summertime cocktails. Lillian and I couldn't have had a better time doing things with Sal and Susan.

Our annual family summer picnic, hosted by Terri and Ken, was another truly epic time. This outing was my family favorite. It gave my entire family a chance to gather for a whole day and long into the evening, with two rounds of barbecue meals and outdoor activities, including a 5k fun run. The side dishes and desserts were amazing. This party signified summer's end, just before the change of season.

Every passing year proved to be better than the years before. I began to work at an asphalt-paving company as their company estimator. The job paid a fair salary. It was a good job, and the owner treated me well. The only drawback was that summer vacations weren't allowed because of the seasonal nature of the business. Lillian and I would make the best of all our spring and summer weekends and took advantage of boating, going to the beach, and overnight getaways whenever we could. We concentrated on saving money, building up our retirement funds.

Throughout the years 2012–2016 we stayed active with running, hiking, boating, and beach going. Lillian had to eventually back off from running, as she was experiencing painful cramping in her calves. We went to several doctors and had several tests done. It was determined that it was most likely caused by a vitamin deficiency. Lillian began to take a zinc supplement, which seemed to help for a year or so, until her doctor finally prescribed a medication to relieve the cramps. This really seemed to work well and slowed down the problem. However, some nights she would jump out of bed in the middle of the night screaming in pain. I was always able to get her calf muscle to relax after massaging it for two to three minutes. It was an intermittent problem and sometimes wouldn't bother her for weeks to months at a time. It was something we learned to live with without any explanation.

One thing that I think holds true for each and every one of us is that we slow down a step or two as we age. This also held true for me and Lillian. Subtle aches and pains took the place of stamina and strength. Outdoor activities seemed to be more challenging, the recovery no longer took minutes, but hours or longer. We laughed about this along with our slightly graying hair. Slow boat rides, walks with our dogs, car rides, dinners out, and small family get-togethers became the new normal for us. Our romantic overtures never slowed. We continued to show our affection for each other and never stopped kissing, hugging, and holding hands. Throughout our lives together we always told each other every morning, every night, and after every phone conversation that we loved each other—no matter what.

When Lillian would be in a conversation with any friends or family members, one phrase that always perked my ears up was when she would refer to me as "her Bobby." It always made me smile. It was always music to my ears. I was and always will be "her Bobby A" until the day I die. We were beginning to fully enjoy our older years together. Both of her kids had completed school and were out on their own, working on their careers. Lillian and I enjoyed being together in the complete privacy of our own home.

During all of our years together our romance and spontaneity never waned. At functions, we would catch each other's eye, smile, and sometimes whisper, "I love you," from across the room. We always seemed to be in our own little world while never looking like it was high school puppy love. I believe that the only person who caught onto our eye contact and connection was my sister,

Terri. She totally understood the vibes between us. In the beginning, Lillian was always a bit intimidated by Terri; not in a bad way, but she would have trouble conversing with her. Lillian once told me, in a kidding way, that she knew Terri was the true head of my family. In time, Terri and Lillian became the best of friends, and I'll always be thankful for their connection and the love that developed between them.

As you are reading this story you might feel that it is totally all about my love toward Lillian, but believe me, she gave me and showed me with her words and actions unconditional love—more than I could ever explain. Lillian came home from work one day telling me about a very kind young lady who worked at the law firm as a college intern. She spoke very highly about her clerical talents and her friendly personality. She said that she would no doubt make someone an awesome girlfriend or, someday, a wonderful wife. Lillian then went on to say that she told the young lady, "I hope that you find a good man to love you as much as my Bobby loves me." That's the wonderful gift that Lillian and I gave each other, the very special warm feeling of deep love that we expressed every day of our lives. It was a truly humbling feeling to know that I was loved and cared for as much as I loved and cared for her.

Many years of our loving journey had now gone by, but yet our love and affection for each other never faded. She still always managed to make my heart go pitter-patter whenever she walked through the door. Even at my age of almost sixty years, I still felt like a young man who was full of vibrant love and romance when it came to my sweet Lillian. We would joke about how our bodies were aging but our hearts and minds were as youthful as the day we met. I still enjoyed the sound of her voice, her soft touch, and sweet lips against mine. In the very beginning of my story I stated that I fell in love with her at first sight, and throughout my life with her it proved to stay true. To me, this beautiful woman could walk on water. She gave me everything I could have ever wanted in life. She filled all the empty voids and completed me totally. When we would witness or hear about couples arguing or fighting, it would bother us. We seldom disagreed or argued, and more importantly, when we did it broke our hearts, and we made things right immediately. Lillian and I always made sure that we never went to bed mad at each other, and we always told each other "I love you" because you never know what each day holds. That's the way we lived our lives together.

Lillian and I had slowed down quite a bit by now. We still enjoyed our neighborhood walks with our dogs and occasional weekends out on our boat at the lake, everything was just slower. We still enjoyed our Friday and Saturday date nights. We would get dressed up for each other and eat at one of our local restaurants. We would go out to pubs, enjoy family dining, or sometimes fine dining. The one thing that I could always count on was sitting across from her, reaching out for her hand, and holding it while—without a single word—as we gazed into each other's eyes, until one of us would finally softly say, "I love you."

One of the restaurants we went to featured a side dish that consisted of fried onions. I hated it, but Lillian always insisted we should get it because she loved it. It was served with some kind of spicy sauce that I didn't like. As I watched her picking at it, I would always pick away at it too. By the time we got home and to bed, my stomach would be on fire, and I would experience the things that go along with that. Lillian would laugh her head off. She still had that zany way about her. Looking back on it now, I think she ordered that awful gut rot just because she knew what would happen. She was still a joker, even after all those years.

Throughout our years, we developed an ear for country music. I guess you could say that we became country music aficionados. For Lillian's fifty-fourth birthday, I surprised her with tickets to a concert with top headliner bands. It was expensive but, I thought, totally worth it. From the moment the first band opened, it was a great show. When the headliner band took the stage, they played two songs and then were forced to stop because of an incoming thunderstorm. This storm turned us off for all outdoor concerts, as it was such a disappointment.

One late spring afternoon, we decided to take our two dogs, Marshall and Molly, to a local freshwater lake in our boat. We dropped anchor for most of the afternoon and had our lunch while our dogs swam around. After hours of relaxation and good conversation, Lillian went to the bow of our boat to pull up the anchor. She let out a painful moan. I jumped up on the bow to help her and asked her what was wrong. She had a pained look on her face. She was holding her stomach and needed help getting up off of her knees. I was scared and headed for the boat launch to load up and go home.

When we got home, her pain had subsided. She decided it was just a muscle cramp and wasn't worth worrying about. I couldn't help but wonder if this was somehow related to the calf cramps that would intermittently happen. For the next month or two I kept our boating festivities to a bare minimum—I didn't want Lillian to have any more problems, but also, I was too scared to see if it might happen again. We shifted our enjoyment to taking weekend field hikes with our dogs or day trips to the beach. I never said anything to Lillian, but I wanted her to be able to enjoy herself without the possibly of getting hurt again.

Typical display
of my love
towards my
sweetheart
Lillian.

Our loving
affection always.

Lillian's second 5-K Run. I was proud of her for getting her first podium finish.

Outdoor dining together in Niantic, CT.

My beautiful
Lillian!

Snowshoeing
in the fields
and woods
where we live.

Lillian operating our boat while salmon fishing on Lake Ontario.

My sweetheart Lillian on the boardwalk at Wildwood, NJ.

Us at one of our
many family
get togethers.

Lillian at
Wildwood
Beach, NJ.

One of our
Sunday morning
field hikes.

Lillian and our
dog, Marshall.

Outdoor dining on the Connecticut shoreline during our weekend visit with my brother Sal and his girlfriend Susan.

My sweet
and
healthy
Lillian
with
her two
brothers,
Ralph
Jr. and
Mickey.

My Lillian,
always upbeat
and positive
during her
long battle.

Our first kiss as
Mr. and Mrs.
Attenello.

Our earlier years
of our loving
relationship.

You may now
kiss the bride.

Our first dance
as Mr. and Mrs.
Attenello.

Our First
Dance on our
very special
wedding day on
July 21, 2018.

On our back
deck just one
month before
her battle ended.
Lillian would sit
on the deck for
hours watching
the birds.

Lillian on her
"Lilly Patio"
during the last
year of her
Journey —
always with
a smile!

Lillian and I in
the Spring of
2020. I pushed
her 3 ½ miles
on a nature
bike path in her
wheel chair.

THE JOURNEY

A very windy day snapped tree limbs leaving debris in our backyard. Both Lillian and I, tired from cleaning up branches, decided to have a quick bite to eat, shower, and head up to bed early to watch TV. While lying in bed watching tv and holding hands, Lillian turned down the volume with the remote. I turned my head toward her and asked, "What's wrong?"

She replied, "Give me your hand." She placed my hand on the side of her right breast and asked me if I could feel a small lump. I told her I couldn't really feel anything, but asked her to explain what she was talking about.

Lillian told me she had been experiencing a dull pain in her right breast and had been feeling a lump for about a week. I told her she needed to make an appointment with her OB-GYN the very next morning, that this wasn't something to be taken lightly. She told me she thought that it might be a pimple or maybe an ingrown hair follicle, but that it didn't seem to be going away.

I didn't get any sleep that night. I just had a bad feeling about it.

The next day Lillian called her doctor and got an appointment for a breast exam for Friday, four days later. The days that followed were stressful, but I wanted to believe it was probably nothing, and I hoped for the best. After all, Lillian was in great shape and stronger than anybody could imagine. What would be the chance that this could be anything to really worry about? We had started back into running—we had run a 5K in our neighborhood a few weeks back, and we both ran at a surprisingly fast pace. We'd gone on frequent Sunday hikes with our dogs. What could go wrong in our lives?

We woke up Friday morning and had our coffee together. We watched the morning news and weather, talked about our weekend plans and dinners we could make. We talked about the possibility of going out to dinner on Saturday night. I confirmed with her the time of her doctor's appointment in our hometown. I told her I'd be there as soon as I got out of work and made a bank deposit. She insisted I shouldn't come because it should be a quick visit, but that if she needed me, she would call me.

I tried not to dwell on it during the day and to concentrate on the demands of my work, but the day felt like it was a month long. Finally, the end of the day came, and I left for the bank. I was at the drive through window about to finish up and pull away when my cell phone rang. I picked it up, expecting it to be Lillian telling me everything was OK.

She was crying. She told me to come to the doctor's office quickly. I asked her what was wrong, and she told me through her tears that they found something, and it wasn't good. I told her I would be there in ten minutes.

When I got to the doctor's office, Lillian was in an exam room getting ready for an ultrasound. The doctor greeted me at the door, took me into his office, sat me down, and told me they had already completed a mammogram. He wanted to explain everything to me. He said, "But first, I want you to know she has a tumor in her right breast about four centimeters below the nipple area."

I walked into the dark room where Lillian lay on the bed with a small sheet over her, surrounded by two nurses and a radiologist, about to begin the procedure. They pointed out the tumor and also showed me that the cancer had spread to a cluster of lymph nodes on the right side of her breast.

I hugged and kissed her and told her we would be OK, that we'd do whatever it took to make it right. She held my arm and said, "Please Bobby, I'm scared."

The doctor took us both into his office and looked right into our eyes. He told us, "Don't worry. It's curable. We'll make an appointment for you to see an oncologist for next week. But first, let's send you to have a biopsy right here in town. They can send the results to the oncologist before he sees you."

That following week we saw a well-known oncologist in the area. The doctor explained that Lillian's cancer was HR positive and R2 negative. The plan was to have her see a surgeon to perform a double mastectomy and remove the cluster of lymph nodes effected by the cancer. Then all would be good. Wow, what a relief! Everything was going to be alright.

The next week we met with the surgeon who was confident about the planned procedure. The oncologist set up a CT scan and bone scan because there was a 12–15 percent chance the cancer could have spread beyond the lymph nodes, but it was highly unlikely. That same week, Lillian had both scans done. We waited through an endless week for the results from the oncologist. Finally, we were called to come down to his office to discuss the results.

Lillian, myself, her daughter Michelle, and her son Chris all went to the appointment. We were expecting to discuss and schedule the upcoming surgery. I remember, while waiting, we were all packed into a small exam room. I was scared and very nervous that something didn't seem right. The doctor was making us wait too long.

Just then the door opened, and the doctor walked in. He asked us all to take a seat. I stood with my arm around Lillian, who sat on the exam table. The room got very quiet and filled with tension. He said, "I have some bad news and some good news. The bad news is the cancer has spread to the bones. It's metastasized and is stage four." At that point, Lillian jumped off the table and tried running for the door. I grabbed her and held her in my arms, soothing her as best as I could.

Then he said, "The good news is your particular kind of cancer is very treatable with hormone therapy and oral chemo pills."

I asked him to be up front and tell us the life expectancy with this kind of cancer. The doctor told us that Lillian was young and in good health, so a ten-to-fifteen-year survival rate was not uncommon.

We all left that meeting feeling numb, scared, panic stricken, and devastated. The one thing I told myself was to stay strong and positive for Lillian. Being positive for her then became my only goal.

The first treatment they prescribed was not tolerated well. We had scheduled a salmon fishing trip in Lake Ontario months before, and Lillian insisted we should still go. It proved to be a mistake. During the trip, the hormone therapy made Lillian's lower back, knees, and hips stiff, and she was in an enormous amount of pain. She could barely walk, sit, or even lie in a bed. My brother, Sal, and his girlfriend, Susan, were on the trip with us and were a big help in taking care of Lillian and keeping her spirits high.

After lunch one day, we received a call from the oncologist's office; he wanted us to come back and see him for more tests. They told us they discovered a small spot or nodule on her spleen. It was like a sucker punch. It seemed like the doctor's approach was to give us good news, and then double down with more bad news. The trip back home was very somber. I couldn't wait to get my sweet Lillian back to our comfortable home where I could start to help her, take care of her, and help keep her spirits high and positive. When we returned back home, I sat down and wrote this short poem:

My Sweet Lillian

I will be with you throughout this journey,
And if you ever get scared, I'll hold your hand.
If you get sad, I'll make you laugh.
If you get weak, I will carry you,
And if you get lost, I'll see us through.
Together we'll hope and pray with faith
That our love will give us much better days.

I hung it on our refrigerator so she could see it every morning and every night, which is where it remained throughout her journey. As time went on, the words of that poem became more significant than I ever would have imagined!

Lillian was given an oral chemo treatment. One day I was at work beginning my first estimate of the day. I received a call from Lillian. While on her way to work, she got so sick she had to pull over on the side of road and was sick to her stomach. I wanted to drop everything and go to her, but she said she was feeling a bit better and was going to continue on to work. She was a real estate paralegal and office administrator for a local law firm. She had worked there for over twenty years. Going back home was not an option in "Lillian's world." Her warrior attitude had already begun to shine as it would throughout her cancer journey.

I was a nervous wreck for the rest of that day. The thing I was quickly realizing was that cancer is a relentless disease that can't wait to take control. In order to combat it, you need all the life altering treatments we see on TV. What they don't tell you is that the side effects can be as bad or worse as the disease itself. It seemed that each day was getting worse for her, not better. As a loved one, you learn to be a caregiver with sadness and the heaviest of hearts. It becomes a way of life that you're forced to deal with each and every day.

I struggled to sleep each night. Every day I was afraid to see what new, unforeseen complications and problems Lillian and I would have to face. A few weeks went by with minimal side effects, including the nausea that came with her treatment. She took medication every six hours to combat the nausea. Some days it worked, others not so much. This was pretty much how her battle went from day one until the end. Good days and bad days were our normal. Over the next few months, Lillian's scans and blood work were stable, followed by good doctor's visits. We had very high hopes that her cancer was stable and under control.

Lillian and I were together twenty years and always

planned on getting married once her two kids had completed college, were living on their own, and set in their careers. When Lillian found out she had cancer she tried to cancel our wedding plans, but I would have no part of it. I loved her too much to let this dreadful disease interfere in our destiny to finally become Mr. and Mrs. Attenello. We started to plan our wedding, and set the date for July 21, 2018.

The upcoming months were exciting and wonderful for us. My whole family was involved with helping to make the arrangements. My sister, Terri, was making our wedding cake; my niece Bonnie was making all the table decorations including the centerpiece for our head table; my niece Kara was making all the place cards for the tables. Everyone was so helpful and happy to help out. I was making the arbor under which we would be married. We both were so excited and happy to finally cross that long-awaited threshold and become husband and wife. Several months before our wedding, Lillian went for one of her every-two-month scans. These were always the most stressful of times. The scan would occur in the morning and the doctor's visit would be late that afternoon. We would both be tense—my fingers would throb all day from my blood pressure being elevated. The days always felt a week long as we waited to see her oncologist. This time, the scan was set for 2:00 p.m., so the doctor's visit was set for 10:00 a.m. the following morning. We headed for his office at 9:30 a.m. The drive was only ten minutes, but I trembled on the ride there every single time. Lillian would never speak; she would hold my hand tightly as I drove.

By the time we were in the small exam room waiting for the doctor to come in, we were always dry mouthed and visibly shaking in anticipation of the results. I would stand next to Lillian with my arm around her, rubbing her back while she sat on the table. I had a physical need to be touching and comforting her during these times. Her children were there during this visit to support her, and I'm glad they were.

The doctor walked in. He leaned against the counter and stared at the floor for half a minute. My jaw dropped. My heart was pounding. Lillian started to tear up. I couldn't stand the suspense; it was tearing me up. I said to the doctor, "Come on, out with it! Just tell us, dammit!"

He looked up and told us he hadn't slept much the night before. He told us the cancer had spread to Lillian's liver. The scan showed a cluster of small spots and a visible tumor. He then went on to say that it was in a small area of the lower liver and the rest of the liver was still healthy. He told us he had ordered a biopsy to see if the cancer had changed into a different genetic form. The next week we went to the hospital to have the biopsy procedure performed.

The biopsy results came back quickly with the same genetic code as the original breast biopsy. The doctor made an appointment to have a port implanted, and Lillian started a new chemo infusion with a new hormone treatment. This came with new side effects for Lillian, including extreme nausea, fatigue, and loss of hair. She began losing her appetite and sense of taste. She would receive treatment every other week with Terri as her support. Lillian referred to Terri as her "chemo buddy."

Several months of scans, blood work, and follow-up doctor's visits had all indicated full stability with the tumor and cancer. We all had high hopes. Lillian and I wanted to complete the planning and preparation for our much-anticipated wedding day. All the invitations had been sent out and all that remained were the final details. Lillian's son Christopher, my brother Sal, and I all went to get fitted for our wedding suits. Lillian had her wedding dress taken in and hemmed. Of course, she wouldn't let me see her in it, but I knew it was going to be as beautiful as she was. We hired a well-known DJ in the area and together picked all the music, including the classic "Wedding March" for when my beautiful bride came down the aisle to the altar. I completed the arbor that was the perfect place for us to begin our married life together.

There were now only two weeks until our big day. I checked off days on the calendar—I couldn't wait. With one week to go, I came home early that Friday and decided to surprise Lillian. I hung white balloons throughout the house with messages on them: "Lillian and Bobby A. 7/21/18," "It's about time!" "True love lasts forever," and "Bobby loves Lillian." When she got home from work that night and saw the balloons, she gave me a big hug and a kiss, and we both held each other and started crying. I wanted her to know just how happy she made me and that I loved her more than anything. I told her, "Thank you, Lillian, for finally becoming my wife!"

That weekend was awesome. We went out to dinner both Friday and Saturday night. We discussed the anticipation and excitement we were feeling about the following weekend. The real countdown began, and soon it was Friday night, the night of our wedding rehearsal.

The tables were set and the centerpieces were all in place. The head table was exactly what we had envisioned. After rehearsal, we held a pizza party at our house. When everyone left, we cleaned up and headed to bed. I couldn't sleep at all that night. I watched her sleep, and I thought to myself, *Sweetheart, you have no idea the perfectly beautiful day you are going to have tomorrow. It's designed for a queen, and that's just what you are, my love.* I lay there in the dark with tears in my eyes thinking, *Why her? Why not me? She's just too kind and has too much left of herself to give to have this terrible disease!*

The next morning, I was up at 5:00 a.m., showered, dressed, and ready to go. I had to meet my sister and brother-in-law at the country club to set up the cake table, and meet the wedding planner to go over the placement of the buffet, the flowers, and all the other last-minute details.

I went back home to suit up. Sal, who was my best man, was there, and together we went back to the country club to meet the photographer. She wanted to take pictures of Sal and me before everyone arrived. The justice of the peace walked up to the arbor, which was set up as the altar, and reiterated where everyone should stand, when to give the rings, and so on. Now it was just me standing up there as the guests started to arrive. My hands were shaking and my heart was pounding. I didn't want to talk; I just wanted to focus on this wonderful ceremony that was about to take place.

Everyone was at their tables and the DJ was playing

soft violin music in the background when I heard someone quietly say, "Here comes Lillian's limo!"

I was lightly trembling with the anticipation of seeing my beautiful bride coming down the white carpet. My granddaughter came down the carpet spraying rose petals and then took her place at the altar. Next came Sal, and he stood right by my side. Lillian's daughter walked down the aisle in a pretty pink bridesmaid's gown. Then all was quiet.

Everyone stood as the "Wedding March" began to play. Lillian and Christopher, who was giving her away, stepped into the room and started down the carpet to the altar. *My God!* I thought. *She's so beautiful, I can't believe she's mine.* I started to tear up. We stood facing each other and recited our vows. We both had tears in our eyes. We had both dreamed of this day for twenty years—now it was finally happening.

Our first dance as husband and wife was Jimmie Allen's "Best Shot." I picked the song because it's no secret that my life with Lillian changed me in so many ways. I am a much better man now than I was before thanks to her and the wonderful love we unconditionally gave to each another. We both cried as we danced. I kept wiping tears from her cheeks while we both quietly laughed. When the dance was over, we returned to the head table with our bridal party and patiently waited for the rest of the festivities to begin.

The food and drinks were plentiful, as this was our special day, and we pulled out all the stops. The DJ kept everyone up on the floor dancing and sometimes acting the fool. Lillian and I couldn't have been happier when we cut the cake that my sister made, which was a seashell-themed cake. It was another beautiful part of our wonderful day.

At the end of the day, Lillian and I stood up at the head table to say thank you and show our appreciation to all our guests. Lillian started crying. I believe that was the moment that she remembered her cancer. Not wanting to see her cry, I cracked a joke that made her laugh. After the reception, we hosted an after-party at our house with additional food and drink, which lasted a few more hours. At the end of the night, Lillian was exhausted from the day and went up to bed, and I stayed up and cleaned.

That Monday was business as usual. Both Lillian and I went back to work. We planned to go to Wildwood, New Jersey, for our honeymoon, but Lillian's health and medical appointments wouldn't allow for it. Instead, we decided to extend the following weekend by taking Thursday and Friday off and planning daytrips as our mini-honeymoon.

The first day we had breakfast out, and then I surprised Lillian by taking her to the car dealership and purchasing her a new jeep. She got to pick every feature she wanted, right down to the rims. The second day we visited Yankee Candle in Greenfield, Massachusetts for lunch and holiday candle shopping, one of Lillian's favorite things. On Saturday we went to Sal and Susan's house down in Niantic at the beach and spent the night. Sal, Susan, Lillian, and I had always got along well and had an unbreakable bond. The day was perfect, with tons of laughter and good food. We had managed to put together a wonderful honeymoon weekend for each other. It wasn't surprising—Lillian and I always had fun whatever we did because we really enjoyed being together. All good things come to an end, and our four-day awesome weekend was over before we knew it.

Monday morning came, and we were back to work. At the end of the day, Lillian and I were still a bit tired from our weekend and went to bed early. I always tried to make sure she got as much sleep as she needed. On Tuesday I was at work writing an estimate when my cell phone rang. It was Lillian's boss. He said, "Bobby, Lillian passed out in our office. We called the ambulance. She's in really bad shape."

I told him to have them take her to Saint Francis

Hospital and that I would meet them there. I called Terri, and we both got to the emergency room at the same time. When I walked into Lillian's room, two nurses and a doctor were working on her. They told me her blood pressure had dropped too low, and they were trying to raise it to a higher level or she could go into cardiac arrest. They were putting an IV into her and injecting medication to raise her blood pressure.

About an hour later her daughter arrived from Boston. We all sat bedside waiting for Lillian's blood pressure to start rising. I went into the lobby to a vending machine to grab a bag of chips. I had Lillian eat about half the bag. I had the thought that the salt might help raise her blood pressure, and within about half an hour her blood pressure came up. Sometimes you need to go with your gut instincts.

The doctor came in and told Lillian they wanted to do a scan of her head, just to make sure the cancer hadn't spread to her brain causing her to pass out. Lillian turned and looked at me, shaking her head *no*. She was phobic about confined spaces. I held her hand and told her to please let them do it; we needed to make sure.

A half hour later they brought her back and told us all was good. The reason for passing out was 100 percent because of the blood pressure medication she had been taking, which she shouldn't have taken while on chemotherapy—the chemo itself lowers blood pressure. They said she was very lucky. I thought, *Her oncologist should have taken her off the blood pressure medication.* I was so frustrated because he knew every medication she was taking and he was the only one who prescribed anything. He should have known better. At that point I lost all respect for him, and more than that, all my confidence in him. In my opinion, he went too fast, had way too many patients, and never paid attention to details. His bedside manner was awful.

I begged Lillian to change doctors, but she wanted no part of that. She felt if it got around that she was a difficult patient, no other doctor would treat her. I kept telling her that wasn't at all true—many patients change doctors for all kinds of reasons. But I also told her I wouldn't stress her out and would support her decision to stay with him. After all, it wasn't up to me. It was really all about what she wanted.

Lillian continued to show her true strength and perseverance. She began to tolerate her chemotherapy much better and started enjoying food again. We took full advantage of her improving health by taking day trips to the beach, going out to dinner, and doing just about anything else she wanted to do. I always told myself that I never wanted to feel like I should have done more or should have taken better care of her throughout her journey. I bought her whatever she wanted. Terri and Ken threw many parties and hosted get-togethers, which Lillian would always enjoy.

We spent a lot of time taking short day trips and sometimes shopping for small things. I always enjoyed these rides. Lillian and I would hold hands the entire time and talk about everyday things. We just loved spending time together. We attempted boating, but it was just too strenuous for her. She cried at the thought of not being able to boat anymore. I kept the boat all through the summer hoping things might change, but unfortunately, everything seemed to get worse. We finally sold the boat that following winter. Lillian referred to our selling of the boat as a part of her already dying.

Our family gatherings and small dinner parties always helped lift Lillian's spirits. I remember one Friday night after we both got home from work, she seemed to be in a very good mood. Her energy and health had been doing well over the past couple of weeks. She asked me over dinner if I would consider taking a road trip to Boston to visit her daughter and check out her new apartment. I thought it through for the rest of our meal and decided that it would be nice for Lillian to take the day trip—it would lift her spirits. I told her, "Of course we can go if that's what you want to do."

The next morning Lillian was up at 6:00 a.m., showered and ready to go. I hadn't seen her excited like this in a very long time. We jumped in her jeep, and off we went. I drove until the last rest stop, then Lillian insisted she drive into the southside of the city where her daughter lived. Reluctantly I agreed, and down the highway we went. Lillian was deathly afraid of trains, planes, tunnels, and elevators. If anyone has ever visited Boston, you know that one wrong turn and you're in a tunnel. Lillian knew that we would have to drive through a long tunnel near Logan Airport. Everything was perfect until she saw the sign to Logan Airport. She stopped the jeep on the left side of the highway by the concrete barriers, the side that is the edge of the fast lane. I asked, "Lillian what the hell are you doing?"

She starting crying. "Bobby please help me. I don't want to go through any tunnels."

I told her that I didn't think I could get out to get to the driver's side. The cars were speeding past us, not more than two feet away. I somehow opened the door just enough to slide out and get to the driver's side as she crossed over the center console of the jeep to the passenger side. What a shit show that was, but we both wound up laughing about it as we were finally safely driving away. Once we arrived at her daughter's apartment, we went out to get a snack at a pub. Her daughter ordered some kind of specialty pizza with bitter green stuff on it and clumps of cheese that smelled awful. Lillian and I forced it down so we wouldn't hurt her daughter's feelings, but we both laughed about how nasty it was, and we both agreed to try not to visit Boston for a long time, if ever again. Lillian and I were a couple of country bumpkins and proud of it. That's why we chose to live in the country, surrounded by farmland and small quiet neighborhood roads.

One thing that both Lillian and I noticed was the number of friends and even relatives we lost contact with after her diagnosis. We had close relatives and a couple of good neighborhood friends that we would often have dinner with or visit for small get-togethers. Many shied away once they heard about Lillian's diagnosis. I don't believe they were trying to be mean, but maybe it was just awkward for them, not really knowing what to say or how to act around Lillian and me during that time. Maybe it was a harsh reality—understanding that it could possibly happen to them; like being around us might bring the curse to their front door. Shame on all of them. It was very hurtful to both Lillian and me. They missed out on furthering the connection we had and sharing additional meaningful moments together. As the saying goes, "I'll forgive, but never forget."

In contrast to that, we had friends we hadn't seen or heard from for a good many years. They heard about Lillian's terminal illness, reached out to us right away, and never stopped giving us wonderful and much-needed support. I will always be thankful to a couple of my longtime friends Norman and Frank. These two guys have been good friends to me for a lot of years and are solid men. They both continuously texted or called me to check on how everything was going and just let me know they were there for us, if needed. That's all Lillian and I ever really needed—to know we weren't completely outcast as though there was a bad case of leprosy within our village. People forget that a terminal illness is fought on two levels: physically and mentally. It has been said that a lot of illnesses, including cancer, are most successfully fought by staying mentally positive. Support from family and friends fuels that very important precious attitude. I believe that was the case for Lillian throughout her battle. Everyone around us told her she was doing well and to never give up; that fueled Lillian's warrior instincts each and every day, even when her back was to the wall and things weren't going so well. She always punched and kicked her way back to center ring, still standing. I often told her to just keep punching and I'll hold "him" still. She never let me down with her internal drive and strength.

I often joked about the fact that I would never tattoo a woman's name on any part of my body unless it was in pencil or washable ink. In July 2018, I designed a very spiritual sleeve tattoo on my right arm. It shows Lillian as an eternal warrior looking down from the heavens toward me as I am kneeling on the ground on one knee with my hand extended, pointing up as if paying a biblical homage to her, my sword stuck in the ground by my side; along with it the words "Eternal Love and Strength Will Live on Forever." My wrist reads "Lillian Strong," and this I am most proud of.

On the night of my tattoo's completion, I told her that I was going to write a book in her honor about her journey throughout her cancer battle. Lillian fell apart and cried as I held her tightly in my arms, also in tears. She told me that she always knew I loved her, but she had never realized the deep magnitude of my love. I had always felt, throughout our years together, that I was the lucky one to have such a special, wonderful, and loving woman to spend each and every day of my life with. It was truly a privilege and honor to be the lucky one that got to be her man.

There were so many challenges for Lillian. Some days she barely had the strength to get out of bed or even out of her recliner, but she always fought through each one of those awfully long and difficult days.

It was at this point that I had a long and much-needed conversation with my boss, who I had been with almost seven years. I explained that I needed to take some time away from my job to take care of my wife. The season was coming to an end in a few more months, and he reluctantly cut my hours back and hired a temporary estimator to cover in my absence. A month or so after our initial conversation, he called and told me that I had to make a decision. He told me that I needed to put his company business first 100 percent and not to bother him with my wife's health condition anymore. My decision was made in less than ten seconds—I thought, *He can go fuck himself.*

From that moment forward, I was home full time and 100 percent Lillian's caregiver. I became her nurse and doctor and provided spiritual guidance. I bathed her when she was too weak, rubbed her down with her favorite lotion, gave her manicures and pedicures. I went to every doctor's appointment, all the treatments, scans, hospital visits, and took her to all her special places when her health would allow it. When she cried, I held her and cried with her. I preached words of encouragement and often cried in the bathroom or outdoors alone. I cooked whatever she could eat every morning, noon, and dinner time. I would stay awake some nights all night long, holding her hand as she tenderly and gently slept. I rarely slept through any night because I would help her to and from the bathroom, if she needed to go. I would administer her medications throughout the night, check her glucose levels, and inject her with the proper dose of insulin. This was because she had developed drug induced diabetes from her chemo treatments. I monitored her oxygen levels and blood pressure. When she was in pain, I would massage her, sometimes for long periods of time until the pain medication kicked in. But the most important thing that I always did every second, minute, and hour of every day, was love her so damn much that she never doubted my heartbroken pain and unconditional love. I will always and forever have that for her. I knew that one day the time would come when I would have to say goodbye to her for the very last time. I was terrified of the thought, but I knew that I must somehow try to prepare myself, if such a thing could be done. Most importantly, I needed to help her prepare by talking about the connection and our biblical and spiritual faith. I knew there would be a time when medical science would fail.

Then her final destiny and fate would fall into God's hands and, sadly, out of mine.

Lillian began to lose a lot of weight. I did everything I could to help her maintain her weight. I made her milkshakes with ice cream and melted peanut butter, adding a half of a banana. I would serve her a pasta dish made with orzo pasta, adding an egg and mozzarella or grated cheese. Pot roast with carrots and potatoes were always a request. I was told early on that it's important that cancer patients maintain a high protein diet, especially while on chemo treatments. I did my best to make sure she followed that regime. As part of my caregiving experience, I learned that when Lillian would go through her extreme-loss-of-weight cycles, the red meat, potatoes, and pasta diet would work the best to slow down the weight loss, but keeping her weight up proved to be challenging.

Lillian developed slight headaches and started to experience blurred vision during certain times of the day. We scheduled an appointment with her doctor, who ordered an MRI. Our biggest fear came to be a terrifying reality. The cancer had spread to her brain—her oncologist described it as a very small spot in a section of her brain. He sent us to a brain oncology specialist who performed a number of tests, including a PET scan. The prognosis from the scan couldn't have been any worse: Her brain had developed small tumors, and the "halo fluids" surrounding her brain were full of cancerous satellite cells, which were very aggressive. The oncologist ordered ten sessions of full brain radiation treatments. The side effects from the radiation treatments were unbelievably and outrageously awful, from hair loss to more extreme fatigue and worsening nausea.

On the morning of treatment number four, Lillian couldn't even walk on her own or dress herself. I laid her on the bed, dressed her, and carried her to the car. When we got to the cancer center, they took a blood draw and learned that her HH level (hemoglobin) was down to 2.2 g/dL. The HH level for Lillian during treatment was supposed to be between 9 and 10 g/dL. She was almost out of blood, like an automobile engine trying to run without oil. She was rushed to the hospital by ambulance.

When we arrived, she was treated very aggressively, like a person would be if they had a fatal gunshot wound. They were pumping units of blood into her, one after another. They were monitoring her blood and oxygen levels as well as her blood pressure. The emergency room was filled with doctors and nurses along with me, her daughter, and my sister. They took additional scans including an MRI and an ultrasound. The doctor came into the room and discussed the results of the tests. Lillian had a ruptured blood vessel in the lining of her stomach. She was losing large amounts of blood and would need surgery right away to repair it. It took two back-to-back endoscopic surgeries to slow down the bleeding. It took several days before the bleeding stopped and her HH levels returned to normal. By the end of her hospitalization, she had received seventeen units of blood.

Three days after she returned home from the hospital, COVID-19 hit. The state of Connecticut went into lockdown, which made Lillian's upcoming doctor's visits impossible to get to. Everything was now virtual, which was, at best, very minimal care. Scans were canceled, hospital appointments were nonexistent. We were all nervous and anxious; we prayed that there would be no unexpected emergencies. In time, everything began to open back up, and Lillian and I were able to proceed with her scheduled medical appointments and scans. Lillian recovered 100 percent from her radiation treatments and the ruptured vessel in her stomach.

Spring of 2020 finally arrived. Lillian and I would spend hours and hours outside on our back deck. She wanted to enjoy the outdoors, as she was tired of being indoors. She told me that being inside felt like she was sitting around waiting for her time to come. In early

April, I found her crying on our family-room couch. I sat down next to her, holding her arm and rubbing her back, and asked her what was wrong. She told me that she would give anything to go for a two mile walk around our neighborhood. I thought about this all day, and then I told her she'd get her walk the very next day. Sunday morning came, and we had our breakfast together. I asked her if she was ready for her much-needed walk. She looked at me with tears in her eyes and told me she couldn't even walk to the end of the short road that we lived on. I looked at her and walked over to her as she sat at our dining-room table. I hugged her and said, "Please Lillian, trust me. You will get your walk in, just as you wish."

We got dressed in our spring jackets and sweatshirts with our COVID-19 approved masks and headed into the Town of Granby, which has a beautiful rail trail that goes on for miles throughout wooded areas. When we got to the parking lot, I pulled Lillian's wheelchair out of the trunk and placed her in it, covering her with a small blanket across her lap, making sure she was warm and comfortable. She smiled and started to tear up once she realized what we were about to do. I pushed my sweet Lillian for almost four miles in her wheelchair. I sang some of our favorite songs to her, cracking small jokes and occasionally stopping to give her a kiss or take a couple of selfie photos of her and I. We shared the best three hours together, and it proved to be something so special. It was so good to see her smile and laugh and in such high spirits. It was times like this when I would feel so honored and privileged to be Lillian's husband and primary caregiver. This was a perfect example of the way I would treat every wish or desire that Lillian had by making it happen and just doing it. I truly enjoyed doing everything I could for my sweet Lillian. My heart bled for her every minute of each and every day. I wanted every minute of her remaining life to be as special and wonderful as I could possibly make it. She absolutely deserved the best loving care I could give her after all that she had done for me throughout our years together. For all these reasons, my very best was what she received each and every day, even as my heart continued to break.

Lillian now enjoyed sitting in a patio chair with a small quilt that she had made. She had worked almost every evening on it until the weakness in her hands made it impossible. My cousin Marie took the remaining material to her house and finished it for Lillian. She would sit, so happy and content, watching me work around the yard, fluffing her flower gardens, and filling up all her bird feeders while country music was playing on our outdoor speakers. One afternoon I had just finished mowing and was putting our lawnmower away in the shed when I noticed out of the corner of my eye Lillian holding onto to our back-deck railing, slowly swaying back and forth to our wedding song, Jimmie Allen's "Best Shot." I stood and watched her from across the yard and cried my eyes out. When the song was over, I walked over to her, with tears in my eyes and helped her back into her chair. We just gazed into each other's eyes, smiling. It was a moment that needed no words to be spoken. There would continue to be constant eye contact between us without any conversation during these final months of her precious life.

About a month before Lillian gave up her battle, she had started to isolate. She would become very quiet and stare off into space with no expression, almost as if she was in a deep trance. When I would ask her if she was OK, she would act as if I just woke her up from a deep sleep. And when I asked what she was thinking, she would reply, "Nothing, just ... nothing really." I realized that this was her very private and, maybe, spiritual process or passage toward what was to be the inevitable—the end of her journey.

Sadness, stress, and disbelief were beginning to firmly take hold of me. I could no longer sleep nor concentrate on anything except for the care of my Lillian. She was so frail and weak. Her appetite was continuing to diminish. She constantly trembled and became unsteady trying to get into and out of her wheelchair. I was nauseous almost every day. It was so heartbreaking to watch my beautiful sweet Lillian slowly slipping away. I knew I would never give up on her. I needed to be her rock, her support, her spiritual guidance. She was still fighting, and I knew that I must fight by her side as hard or even harder than she was.

Lillian's smiles and humor started gently slipping away. There was a slight air of tension throughout the house. Never with each other, but more like the dread of the unknown—when and how it was going to end. I could only think, *How bad will my sweetheart suffer? How much more pain can she deal with?*

Lillian would lie next to me in bed at night holding my hand as I would softly stroke her arm and watch her stare at the ceiling. She was probably thinking about how much time she might have left. She would often ask me questions about my religious beliefs and my theory on life after death. I realized I needed to help her reconnect with her spiritual beliefs. It was a cold uneasy feeling, but I came to realize that her time might be coming soon.

One night, Lillian told me that when she was gone, I needed to be strong and get back in touch with my own identity. She told me to get back to all the things we used to do together—hike, run, workout; to be the "Bobby A" she fell in love with. She ordered me to not sit home grieving my life away, but to get out, be social, take companionship. She said, "Don't spend your life being bitter, angry, or miserable."

I stopped her right there and told her, "Don't talk like that, we need to focus on now, not the after."

She raised her voice and said, "Dammit Bobby, I want you to become that Bobby I know and love."

I teared up, nodded my head, and told her, "I'll figure it out when the time comes." I told her I would first need to learn how to live my life without her. I said, "No one will ever have my heart. It will always belong to you. I will truly belong to only you forever." As time went on, Lillian would engage in more of these intimate "when I'm gone" conversations.

She blindsided me one afternoon by saying, "Bobby, I finally figured out the final piece of my life puzzle." She went on to say, "You were sent to me not just as my loving soulmate, but by God himself as my guardian angel."

I responded with, "Come on, Lillian, you're going to make me cry."

She continued to say, "I'm really serious, no one could have ever loved me as much as you with such loyalty and dedication. And absolutely no one could have given me the constant high level of care these past few years, as you have but a true guardian angel. Because of all of this, I truly believe that you are a guardian angel sent to me by God himself."

I hugged her and kissed her and thanked her for her kind words. I then walked into our bathroom and broke down and cried. I couldn't imagine how alone she must be feeling during this precious time of her life. I realized that God was starting to whisper in her ear.

The following week was another appointment to get a scan. The past few weeks, Lillian had developed a small cough every evening. Her doctor felt it was a case of allergies or perhaps postnasal drip, but nonetheless, he wanted to err on the side of caution.

Lillian's oncologist Facetimed us to discuss the results later that afternoon. He started off by asking how she was feeling. Lillian asked him about the results of the scan, and he told her the scan didn't look good. He went on to say that the cancer had spread into her left lung with many spots and several sizable tumors. It needed to be drained the next day at the hospital because there was so much fluid in her lungs. He told us that she didn't have much time left. This is a perfect example of why I disapproved of him as Lillian's doctor—his bedside manner was nonexistent. I felt that there was no need to upset Lillian further with that declaration when she was already devastated by the outcome of her scans.

The next morning, we left for the hospital early to have her lung drained and a catheter implanted for future drainage. This procedure was called thoracentesis and pleurodesis along with the insertion of a PleurX drainage system, which was to be drained once a week at home. Lillian did well with this new treatment; her cough went away and her spirits remained high. Visiting nurses came once a week to drain her lungs, and they allowed me to assist them when needed. Her cancer had spread to her liver, spleen, bones, brain, and now her lungs. It had completely taken over her body. I needed and wanted to do more for her; I felt so helpless.

I began to focus on her spiritual guidance, coached her to believe in her faith to reconnect with all her religious beliefs. I made an appointment with our priest from Sacred Heart Church to visit Lillian at our home. Monsignor Clancy and Lillian had a wonderful connection right from the start. He made her laugh and smile as they talked and reminisced about the area that she grew up in. She received the Anointing of the Sick. The monsignor commented on her strength and positive attitude. He told Lillian that she had more life in her than he expected to see. I credit that to the warrior strength that she maintained throughout her whole battle.

The monsignor met with Lillian two more times, and after each visit, she would feel spiritually lifted and very happy they met. There was more of a peaceful calm about her. She was a little less anxious.

I remember one very significant conversation Lillian and I had regarding her passing. She was very calm as she began to explain to me that she fully believed and understood that she would eventually pass away, most likely in a very short amount of time. She went on to tell me how scared she was, so I held her tightly in my arms and told her that she would be going to a better place, a place of complete tranquility, of an eternal spiritual life. I said, "You will be whole again just as you were before you became terminally ill." I went on to say that she would be free of all her pain and suffering, and she would join all her family, friends, and loved ones who had passed before her. I also explained to her that it would be a harsh reality for those she would leave behind. I would grieve deeply and with the heaviest of hearts, but she would soar among angels who await her arrival. However, she would have to leave us behind, and that was truly the sad part of my belief.

The following weekend Lillian asked to go down to

the beach to visit Sal and Susan. They had a beautiful day planned for us. We went down to their private beach and set up Lillian in a nice, shady location in a comfortable lounge chair. Susan walked with her to the edge of the water up to her tiny ankles so she could watch my brother and I clamming about twenty yards out. We kept staring and glancing at each other with tears in our eyes. I think we both knew this was more than likely her last trip to Niantic and possibly the last time she would see Sal and Susan.

At the end of the day, we went back to their house. Susan had made us a nice meal, but Lillian couldn't eat. She had no appetite. Sitting down to a home cooked meal was becoming a thing of the past. At home, I made her smoothies and soup and sometimes she could force down a small bowl of cereal. The visit was calm and relaxing. Sal and Susan were always warm and welcoming, and for that I'll always be thankful.

On the ride home, I put the passenger seat back so Lillian could rest and relax. I held her hand softly and with tears in my eyes I sang "Home Sick" by Kane Brown. I was trying to tell her, through the song, that I would be heartbroken when she's gone because my heart would always belong with her. When the song was over, I turned to look at her, and she was softly crying as she gazed out the passenger-side window. The rest of the ride home was very quiet with very little conversation. The only sound was the country music playing. It became very clear to me that this trip down to the shoreline was Lillian's way of saying goodbye to two people that she had loved and adored for so many years; who we had shared good times and fond memories with that we would all hold in our minds and hearts forever.

Two months before Lillian's journey came to an end, a good friend of hers lost his long battle with cancer. When I reluctantly told her, I was afraid how it would affect her in her courageous battle. To my surprise, she handled it fairly well. However, it really upset her, and she broke down and cried as I held her in my arms. The next day she asked me when the service would be. I told her it was scheduled for the following week, but family members suggested she not go due to her health conditions. When I told her that, she struggled her way out of her chair, stood up, looked me right in the eye, and said, "Fuck them and you too, I'm going."

The next day, I took her shopping and bought her a black dress that would fit her now frail body. The evening of our friend's wake, Lillian asked if we could stand together on our back deck, and she had her daughter take a picture of us. I helped her out to our car, and we left for the funeral home. On the ride, there was complete silence, and Lillian had tears streaming down her face. I knew that this was going to be very difficult for her for a lot of reasons. I think she felt loyalty, but I'm also sure she felt that it was a look into her own ending.

Once again, Lillian proved herself to be the strongest person I've ever known. I helped her into her wheelchair, and we headed into the service. When we walked in, we were greeted with open arms by family members, and both Lillian and I had tears in our eyes. I was so very proud of her, attending this wake, knowing it had to be one of the toughest things for her to do. I'll never forget how his wife stepped away from her position in the receiving line, knelt down, and gave my sweet courageous Lillian a hug as they both cried. I'll always remember that very warm welcome, and that everyone gave my wife the respect that she no doubt deserved.

The next day, I came home from running errands and walked into the living room to give Lillian a hug and a kiss. She excitedly told me to go look at the gift she had gotten for me that was on the dining-room table. It was the picture of both of us taken on the back deck from the day before, in a pretty white frame. I started to cry as I hugged her and thanked her for the tender thoughtfulness that went into this gift. She wiped the tears from my eyes and asked me to do her a favor. She asked me, "Please put this photo up where you'll always see it every day, and please do it very soon so I can see where it will hang." I hung it over our family-room TV, which is where it will always stay.

I began to notice that both our dogs, Marshall and Molly, who were Lillian's babies, stayed by Lillian's side all day and night. When she was in bed, they would sleep by her side. When she was in the shower or bathroom, they would wait outside the door. This went on every day. I felt a bitterly sad feeling deep inside of me. I have always believed that animals have very strong internal instincts for life-ending sicknesses. I asked myself, "Could they be doing this kind of behavior because Lillian's time is near?" I felt sick to my stomach, and my hands would tremble at the thought of it all.

I believe that Lillian felt the same way. Several weeks before she ended her battle, she had a long conversation as we lay in bed holding hands, watching TV. She reached over to turn the volume down. She said, with tears in her eyes, "Bobby, I know that when I pass away I will no doubt be going to a better place, free from all my pain and suffering, but I don't want to leave you. I love you too damn much."

She broke down and cried uncontrollably as I hugged and kissed her, rubbing her back and crying on her shoulder. All I could say was, "Lillian, I just don't know how I'll exist without you."

Lillian was just beginning to show many signs of weakness. Most of her days and nights would be spent sitting quietly in her favorite recliner or napping in bed. Cancer was starting to win over her, wear her down, physically and mentally. But still I knew my sweetheart, Lillian. I knew how she thought, felt, and even how she reacted to things. I knew she wasn't done fighting yet. She was on borrowed time, but wasn't giving up her battle. Proving again to be a special warrior!

ENDING HER BATTLE

July 21st was our two-year wedding anniversary, and Lillian wanted to make it to this day more than anything. We were invited to Terri and Ken's house, where my niece Bonnie had made an awesome homemade cake for us. We all had a wonderful time with plenty of food and lots of laughs as always. My beautiful, sweet Lillian was so weak, but still managed to be part of the fun-filled occasion. That was just her nature—to always be fun, with a warm smile. She loved being with my side of the family. Only when the day was over did I realize how tired she really was. I had to help her get to the car and then pick her up and put her into the seat. As usual, she being the warrior she was, she made it through the day and managed to celebrate our very special event.

In the days that followed, Lillian's stomach began to

grow fully distended and needed to be drained to relieve the pressure. Her doctor scheduled an appointment to have it drained. This proved to be a temporary fix only; the uncomfortable procedure now needed to be done once a week. As always, Lillian showed her true strength and positive attitude, and she pressed on week after week at these appointments.

She set her next goal: to make it to my birthday, August 2nd.

One night during the last week of July, Lillian got out of our bed without waking me up and tried to make it to the bathroom on her own. She lost her footing and fell. I jumped up and freaked out, shaking. I picked her up, helped her to the bathroom, and then back to our bed. I checked her from head to toe for cuts or bruises, but thank God, she was OK. The next morning, I decided we would now stay on the ground floor. I made our living room into a makeshift bedroom. There was a full bathroom with a handicap shower that I had built for when Lillian needed it. She had been adamant that she would not sleep downstairs as long as she could make it up and down from our bedroom with my assistance.

At this time, she began using a walker. For the next several nights we slept downstairs, and she showered in the handicap bathroom with my help. Her treatment caused her blood sugar levels to spike one evening, several days before my birthday. I went to get her insulin injection. When I came back to the living room, she looked directly at me with tears in her eyes and said, "Bobby, I can't do this anymore."

I felt the blood drain to my feet, and I started to tremble. I asked her to please explain what she meant. She cried, apologizing to me, and said, "I'm done fighting. Please don't be mad or disappointed in me."

I told her I could never be disappointed in her, that most people couldn't have fought as long as she did. I then said that I would support her decision no matter what, but I asked her to sleep on it. I knew once she decided to end her battle mentally, she would quickly fail physically, so I told her I would ask her again in the morning.

The next morning, I was awake at 5:00 am. When Lillian woke up a couple of hours later, I asked her for her final decision. She said, "I'm done battling. I'm at peace with passing on. I'm going to a better place, and I need you to be strong and understanding." I promised her I would take care of her until the end.

We discussed the hospice preparations and about stopping treatment. We began making all the nursing arrangements and canceled her upcoming doctor's appointments and scans. We dismissed her oncologist.

The hospice people were great. A nurse was there the very next day to help us come to terms with Lillian's end-of-life plan. A hospital bed was moved in and pain management began. I felt sick to my stomach. My legs were shaking, and I couldn't believe her time was coming to an end.

I couldn't stop the angry and endless string of thoughts in my head. *What about us? What about spending our golden years together? What about the love we share for each other? What about everything we worked for, the house, the dogs, our kids, and family? And how will I survive without my true love, my friend, my companion, and soulmate, this beautiful woman I'll be in love with forever? We're not done! We have too much to offer each other!*

"Please God," I begged, "Not yet! Give us more time, please, don't take her!" I was in total shock and numb, as if I was living out a bad dream.

As the day went on, the reality started to sink in. Our next-door neighbor and very good friend Sue came over. Sue has participated in life-ending caregiving several times with close friends and family members. She could see that I was in shock and denial, and she knew that I was close to coming unraveled. Sue had my back and helped me to understand what the upcoming days would entail. She stayed with me, coached me, helped me to take care of Lillian, attended meetings with the hospice team, and even cooked and brought meals over to us every day, forcing me to eat. She was an angel sent to help me in the saddest, most heartbreaking, and toughest time of my life. Mrs. Pat, another longtime friend of Lillian's and also a neighbor, came over every day. She gave us a small book to read called *Gone from My Sight*, which helps explain the dying experience. I read it twice. I couldn't believe that everything that was in the book was something I had already experienced with my own eyes or was watching unfold with each passing hour.

On the first official day of hospice, Lillian's jaw tightened, and she had to speak through her clenched teeth. By the end of the day, her voice changed from a normal voice to one of a feeble older lady. By day two, her eyesight failed. She could no longer focus on anything or any one of us. By that night, she either kept her eyes closed, or they were rolled back into the back of her eyelids. All I could do was keep going into another room, outside, or into our master bedroom and cry.

On day three of hospice, she was almost 100 percent bedbound and needed to be diapered in case she had an accident while she slept. Lillian would wake up and let out a soft screech or grunt to get my attention so I could bring her to the bathroom. I would lift her out of bed onto her wheelchair, then lift her onto the commode, then back to the wheelchair and back into bed. This routine continued almost every hour all through the night and into the next morning. I noticed that she wasn't doing anything while on the commode. I asked her if something, someone, or anything was scaring her or making her feel uneasy while she was in bed. She nodded her head *yes*.

My God. I then fully realized she was slowly leaving us. It was like she was having an out-of-body experience, as if something was calling her from beyond. But she was still fighting it. She just wanted to go into the bathroom to get away to a safe place. I now stayed by her bed almost all the time, holding her hand and softly talking to her when she would flinch and moan in her sleep. Lillian now slept most of the time. No more bathroom calls, no more screeching, few movements of any kind. Her breathing was through an open mouth with short breaths.

I now sat in total silence, very weary from a lack of sleep. The room was quiet with country music playing softly in the background. The tranquil environment was broken by the sound of a phone ringing. When I answered, I heard James's voice asking if he could come over to visit Lillian. James was Bobby Jr.'s brother-in-law, a Green Beret in the Army. He was on his way back to Connecticut from the military base where he was stationed. I explained that

Lillian was no longer coherent, but he insisted. He wanted to see her and say goodbye. Both Lillian and I had a very strong connection with James, he was a very special friend and loyal relative through my son's marriage. He has seen his fair share of war and has been in rough situations, but he's always persevered.

Several hours later, James arrived and quietly walked into the room with a small bouquet of flowers. He sat down in a chair beside Lillian's bed where she lay peacefully sleeping. I watched as he softly held her hand with tears in his eyes. I thought, *What a remarkable man he is.* It showed yet another example of how many people loved and respected my wonderful, sweet Lillian. She touched the hearts of everyone who knew her. After a few minutes, James slowly stood up and leaned over Lillian to whisper goodbye, gave her a gentle kiss on the forehead, and slowly walked away.

By day four, I was done eating, drinking, or even thinking straight. I was so full of grief I felt as though I was the one having an out-of-body experience. Throughout the past couple of days, I felt like I was going to be sick to my stomach at any minute. My heart was pounding in my chest. My hands wouldn't stop shaking. I kept kissing her cheek and crying, whispering in her ear how much I loved her, telling her I'll always be her "Bobby A." I sat bedside with her through the night or sat in the recliner at the foot of her bed.

On day five, Sal came into town to stay with me. He got the news Lillian was near her end and also knew I wasn't doing well. The hospice nurse held a meeting with us and told us it wouldn't be much longer. She showed us how Lillian's feet and hands were becoming purplish, and she was becoming very blotchy on her arms and other areas.

Our house was now full of family and friends who were very close to both Lillian and me—her two kids, her son's girlfriend, my brother, Sue, Dave, John. It was very tense, but yet some kind of calm was taking hold. That evening, we were all gathering around her in chairs and taking turns softly stroking her arms and hands, hoping she could still feel our presence and our love. We were taking shifts, one or two of us at a time, to mill around the house for five or ten minutes.

At one point it was my turn to walk around the house for a minute to stretch my legs. I was talking to Sue's husband, Dave, in the kitchen, and at the end of our conversation I excused myself and told him I wanted to be with my Lillian. When I returned to the living room, I went over to the side of the bed and softly placed my left hand on Lillian's hair; I began stroking it while holding and stroking her hand with my right hand. I was leaning over her, softly kissing her on her cheek and forehead, whispering in her ear to relax. "I love you, I'm here," I said. "It's OK, it's time to go to all your friends, family, and loved ones in heaven. God's calling you. Always know I'll love you forever and will always be your 'Bobby A.' I'll have you in my heart, and I'll never, ever forget you. You can go now. I'll be strong, and I'll be OK."

I picked my head up and looked around the room. Everyone had tears in their eyes. I kept stroking her, kissing her, and whispering to her. I could see and hear her breathing soften and then stop as she lay on the pillow with her eyes half open, looking right at me. I knew she was gone.

When I stood up, I felt my knees give way, and I let out a loud scream. How it happened I don't know, but Sal was there, holding me up and hugging me and crying along with me. He kept saying, "Go ahead, brother, I got you. I'm not letting go. Cry it out, it's OK. I got you!"

When I regained my composure, I told everyone in the room I wanted to give Lillian a sponge bath, rub her favorite lotion on her, remove the sensor for reading her sugar levels, and dress her in her favorite pajamas and slippers. I told everyone that she wasn't leaving until she was beautiful and dignified. I closed her eyes and kissed her lips gently. Lillian's daughter and Sue and I did everything the way I wanted. Her daughter even painted her finger nails pink, which was Lillian's favorite color. I put the beautiful quilt Lillian had made several months ago, which was finished by my cousin Marie, over her, leaving her arms on top, as if she were sleeping. I called everyone back into the room to gather around my lovely Lillian.

I said the Lord's Prayer, and I asked Him to please take her into His arms and let her soar to the heavens to be with all of her loved ones, family, and friends who had gone before her, amen.

I contacted both hospice and the funeral home. Within half an hour, the nurse from hospice came to pronounce Lillian's passing: August 5, 2020, at 11:06 p.m., three days after my birthday.

A short time later, the team from the funeral home came to take my beautiful wife away from me and from the home we had worked so hard to create. I was trembling and crying as I watched her leave our home for the very last time.

The following week, we held Lillian's wake and funeral, which I had preplanned and designed down to the last detail. All six pallbearers were on point, with James dressed in full military uniform at the head of the casket. The church echoed with our special song, Kenny Chesney's "Better Boat." I completely fell apart thinking of our slow dance to it and Lillian's words for me to be strong after she was gone. I remembered her telling me with tears in her eyes, "Bobby, you need to rebuild your life and build a better boat!" Then she'd asked that I play this special song at her funeral as gift from her to me.

Monsignor Clancy gave her a wonderful and heart-filled eulogy. He reflected back to the several visits he had with her. He referred to her as a very interesting and courageous woman who was very giving of herself to everyone who was in her life. He mentioned the love and connection that she and I had for each other. The monsignor went on to talk about the teachings and impressions that she had made on many of us throughout our lives. He told us that no doubt she was now free from all her pain and in a better place. He suggested the best way to honor her legacy was to take the one thing that she taught or showed us that affected us and carry it on throughout our lives.

Several family members and close friends stood up and presented their reflections and read personal eulogies. They all seemed to point to the same theme, which was the deep unconditional love and devotion Lillian and I had for each other. The one reading that was the most impactful was from my niece Kara. She read:

> My uncle Bob asked me to say a few words about Lillian, but instead I am going to talk about them as a couple.
>
> My uncle has always been a bit of a loose cannon. He's got an Italian temper, he's got a foul mouth, and he has given my two teenage sons some of the most wildly inappropriate advice you can imagine.
>
> In my eyes, Lillian tamed my uncle Bob ... but not in the way you'd think. She didn't tame him the way a trainer tames a wild animal. She never tried to restrain him or alter his behavior.
>
> Lillian tamed him in a much older sense of the word. In Shakespeare's day, the word "tame" meant "to break something open." Back then, alcohol was stored in giant clay vessels, and to break them open, you had to strike the top with a stick or a sword. So "taming" a vessel meant breaking it open to get to the good stuff inside.

And that's how Lillian tamed my uncle. She brought out the really good stuff.

This was true throughout their entire relationship for sure, but it was especially true in these last few years, when he gave himself up completely to her care, becoming her husband and her doctor and even her spiritual advisor when she needed it. Lillian taught my uncle that he is capable of more than he ever knew because he was loved by her so unconditionally. It's exactly the way he loved her back. And together, it's the bar they set for the rest of us.

When Kara finished reading her eulogy, the church was so quiet that you could hear a pin drop. I became very emotional with tears streaming down my face, but I was so happy that my niece realized the deep love that Lillian and I shared for one another. At that moment, the monsignor called out, "Lillian's husband, Bobby, would like to say a few words."

I wiped my tears away, cleared my throat, and slowly walked to the podium. I gazed out over my wonderful family and friends, who all had tears in their eyes. As I gathered my composure, I remembered that many of my family members had advised me not to try to read my personal eulogy. They all thought it would be too emotional and hard on me. I took a deep cleansing breath, and I began to speak:

> Let me tell you about my wonderful wife, Lillian.
>
> Lillian was kindhearted, full of strength, and always had total conviction for whatever she did. She taught me to be a better man; to think everything through; to be kinder; and most of all, to love softly, consistently, and unconditionally.
>
> During the past three years, Lillian showed me how to remain positive throughout the most challenging times in her life. She showed her true warrior strength during the most difficult times of her battle. I'll always remember a conversation we had several months ago. She said, "Bobby! I finally figured out the last piece of my life's puzzle." She went on to say, "You were sent to me by God himself, not just as my soulmate, but as my true guardian angel." She continued

to go on by saying "No one man could have ever loved me as much as you have. Only a guardian angel could have ever taken care of me to the extreme level of care that you have these past few years!" At that time and moment, I realized that her time was coming near, and God himself was now starting to whisper in her ear.

So now I say to you, my beautiful little warrior, it's now your time to soar to the heavens above; to be with God and all your loved ones who passed before you. I salute you for all that you have done for me. You will always and forever be in my heart, until we meet again. I will love you forever and will always be your "Bobby A."

When I finished my eulogy, I slowly walked to Lillian's casket, I stood at full attention facing the casket with my back to all the wonderful people who attended the funeral. Monsignor Clancy stood at the front of the altar facing me, with his eyes focused on mine as I gave a formal military salute to my sweet Lillian, showing true honor to her courageous warrior spirit and the wonderful love that we shared for the best twenty-three years of my life.

At the end of the church service, we walked behind her casket. I thought, *This is the end of any connection with her in this earthly world. I'll never have any opportunity to see her in the flesh again.* My knees weakened, and I cried uncontrollably.

My brother walked behind me and rubbed my shoulders and back while my daughter walked by my side, holding my hand. Again, Sal said to me, "I got you, brother. I'm here," as he, too, cried.

As we all stood behind the hearse, I watched the pallbearers carefully place her casket inside. Then they closed the door. I finally realized I had been blessed to spend the best twenty-three years of my life with the most beautiful and wonderful woman that you could ever imagine. I was somehow chosen to be her lover, soulmate, best friend, and most importantly, her caregiver for the final three years of her precious life, which allowed me to see *Her Journey through My Eyes.*

Now I'm trying to pull my life together, as I promised Lillian that I would in so many conversations. I am not completely alone. I have her ashes in a beautiful urn on our fireplace mantel, and I'm surrounded by many hanging pictures of Lillian and me. I say good morning and good night to her every single day. I'll forever love and miss my beautiful wife, Lillian. I vow to live each day throughout my life in honor and loving memory of her.

I have shed many tears while writing this story. But I felt it needed to be written, as it was a promise I made to Lillian as part of her legacy. I say to my sweet Lillian:

> I breath in, I breathe out,
> I ride the waves I can't control.
> If it's working, I don't know.
> When I get done, the thing may not float,
> But I'm learning how to build that better boat.
> I love you honey, wherever you are!

God bless all who read my book. I hope you enjoyed it and that it in some way resonated with you. And may your internal spirit guide you to a better life.

Sincerely,
Robert F. Attenello
a.k.a. "Lillian's Bobby A!"

In the true spirit of my story, *Her Journey through My Eyes*, I encourage you to please listen to the following songs, which all have a meaningful significance.

1. Our first-dance wedding song was Jimmie Allen's "Best Shot."
2. Our slow dance at home just several months before my Lillian passed away was to Kenny Chesney's "Better Boat," which was played at her funeral, per Lillian's request.
3. I sang Kane Brown's "Homesick" to Lillian as I held her hand on the ride home from her last trip to the CT Shoreline.
4. "Got What I Got" by Jason Aldean was softly playing in the background during Lillian's passing.

The referenced booklet is *Gone from My Sight*, by Barbara Karnes.

The cover photo is Lillian's favorite print, "Mocha Wall Peppers," 530551 Germany Scrubia, mocha.org, Grass Bridge Free Images.

Thank you to all.

MEET MY JOURNEY FAMILY

Avery Sherrill: Research and Social Media Management

Karen Barrows: Editor in Chief, Manages Submission to Publishing

Miriam Malone: Longtime friend in charge of typing and electronic filing.

ABOUT THE AUTHOR

Robert F. Attenello (Bobby) has always had a passion for creative writing and poetry. He's very spiritual, but has a slight rough side to him as he is a lifelong construction worker. His deep love for his wife has inspired him to complete his desire to publish his writing. His debut as an author is *Her Journey Through My Eyes*, the true love story of him and his wife Lillian.